POEMS BY WANG WEI

POEMS
by
WANG WEI

translated by

Chang Yin-nan

and

Lewis C. Walmsley

CHARLES E. TUTTLE COMPANY
Rutland, Vermont   Tokyo, Japan

European Representatives

For the Continent :
BOXERBOOKS, INC., London

For the British Isles :
PRENTICE-HALL INTERNATIONAL, INC., London

Published by the
Charles E. Tuttle Company
of Rutland, Vermont & Tokyo, Japan
with editorial offices at
15 Edogawa-cho, Bunkyo-ku, Tokyo

Library of Congress Catalog Card
No. 58-7723

First printing, 1958
Fifth printing, 1963

Book design and typography by
Roland A. Mulhauser

Printed in Japan

CONTENTS

POEMS OF FOUR SIX-CHARACTER LINES

POEMS OF EIGHT
FIVE-CHARACTER LINES

POEMS OF EIGHT
SEVEN-CHARACTER LINES

IRREGULAR POEMS,
FIVE-CHARACTER LINES

IRREGULAR POEMS, SEVEN-CHARACTER LINES

ILLUSTRATIONS

The end papers show the first and last portions of
a long horizontal scroll attributed to Wang Wei,
entitled, *Clearing after Snowfall on the Mountians along
the River.* It is possibly a 17th or 18th century
copy. Formerly in the collection of Lo Chên-yü,
Tientsin. Courtesy, Alice Boney, New York.

The design on the title page was taken from a drawing by Chang Ta-ch'ien, an outstanding modern
artist.

PREFACE

So far as we are aware only a few of the poems of Wang Wei have been translated into the English language. Of the hundred and thirty-six compositions included in this volume about thirty have appeared in previous collections. Our version of these poems has been included in the present edition because our interpretation would seem to differ sufficiently from other translations to merit consideration.

Most of the poems in the present selection have been taken from *Wang Yu-ch'eng Chi Chien-chu* (Complete Works of Deputy-minister Wang, with Commentaries and Notes). This edition, based on a much earlier work edited by Ku Chi-ching in the Yüan Dynasty A. D. 1280–1368, was arranged in twenty-eight volumes by Chao Tien-cheng and published in 1736. The rest of the poems included herein were chosen from *Wang Wei Shih* (Poems of Wang Wei) edited by T. W. Fu and published by The Commercial Press, Shanghai, 1930.

The Romanization followed is "a slightly modified adaptation of Wade's *Syllabary*" found in Matthew's *Chinese-English Dictionary*. In certain geographic names a common form of Romanization has been used.

This present collection contains most of Wang Wei's shorter verses and several of his longer poems on nature and on stories from history. Although Wang Wei is noted also for poems eulogistic of the emperor and of high officials, they have been omitted because they lack the natural beauty and "inner refreshment" of his briefer and more spontaneous compositions.

Wang Wei achieved as much fame as an artist as he did as a poet, but unfortunately no authentic work of his remains. However it was the practice of early artists to copy the old masters and among these still survive a number of paintings "after Wang Wei." Since they in all probability represent something of Wang Wei's own style, several of them have been included in this present work. A few other paintings which seem particularly to illustrate the mood of a poem have also been added.

Our deep appreciation is extended to Catherine Chang and Constance Walmsley for their encouragement and inspiration; to Leslie Kilborn for sending material from Hong Kong; and to Miss Lin T'ung-yü both for copying the texts of Wang Wei's poems and for valuable suggestions offered.

Especially do we thank Dorothy Hamilton Brush whose poetic gift and capacity to catch the instant mood have left a trace on many a line.

Chang Yin-nan
Lewis C. Walmsley
University of Toronto
Toronto, Canada

INTRODUCTION

The poetry of Wang Wei, intimately personal in character, may well be likened to a diary of the human spirit. Let, then, this introduction also be of a personal nature. Let me attempt to convey something of the adventure in joy shared by Chang Yin-nan and myself while translating the following poems. For him, our work has eased somewhat the nostalgia within his heart caused by long exile from his native land. For me, it has been an exultant escape : through the doorway of the mind, I have walked away from concrete city blocks to roam the spacious Chinese countryside once more. Both of us were happily forced back in spirit to the world of nature.

Simply, poignantly, Wang Wei relates his reactions to " the ten thousand problems that pursue our life, " depicting the basic significance of experience against a multicoloured back-drop of surpassing natural beauty. In order to catch his elusive moods and meanings, we have been obliged often to " stand still, and wait and listen, " until we could share his thinking, see what he saw, and feel what he felt. A pleasant task—made less difficult because both Mr. Chang and I lived many years in China before the Communists took control.

There we fell heir to the timeless atmosphere of the poet's day, little changed by the centuries. Like Wang Wei, we each made pilgrimages to the sacred mountains; we each meditated with the hermits; we, too, were irresistibly drawn into the heart-beat of the earth which pulses in natural beauty. Like Wang Wei, we watched spring garments being fitted to the weeping willows as their swaying branches brushed the jade-cool pathways; we, too, have swept up before our own doorways the ever-drifting pink petals of the flowering peach; and in the fresh dawn we have gazed at early blue smoke curling in mountain mist above little houses in an awakening village . . . We, too, have passed through the mountain storms, mindful only of recurrent flashes of ominous lightning—but there, we are stealing thunder from the poet!

In venturing this translation, Mr. Chang and I have been made all too aware of the advantages a poet in Chinese has over the relatively limited English language. A scope, a freedom exists, scarcely comprehensible to those acquainted only with English. With no rigid rules of grammar, with little concern for tense, number or mood, the Chinese author can skip blithely along, indeed fly. Like rabbit's foot-prints in new-fallen snow, his fresh impressions follow one another in crisp, staccato form. The pictographs are so intriguing and the reward from solving them is so satisfying that the translator becomes a fascinated addict who must ever pursue the mystery.

Western readers may find sometimes a lost line or two which may seem an unrelated idea, a nonsequitur.

This may be explained by Wang Wei's unstudied naturalness. Spontaneous thinking or conversation seldom produces a logically connected expression. At the same time, if the imagination probes beneath the apparent break, the reader can usually fill in the jump in thought.

The utter simplicity of Wang Wei's poems is the opposite extreme of the complexity and abstruseness of our so-called modern poetry.

Chinese poetry is three-dimensional. In modern terms, it compares with English poetry as television with radio; for it appeals not only to ear and mind, but to the eye as well. Each character portrays an impression, an insight into experience, a thought. The Chinese scholar or lover of poetry extracts much more meaning from watching the characters as he sings them aloud than he does from only hearing them read. There is no exact equivalent for this third-dimensional value in the rendering of English poetry—even though today certain modern poets who chant their poems do add interest to them.

A single Chinese character will often condense the meaning of many words in English. Take the character 閒, *hsien*, for instance: the ordinary dictionary defines it as "leisurely, quiet, unoccupied." Take the symbol apart, and a great deal more is disclosed. It is made up of two main parts: two doors opening from the centre, 門, and the moon, 月, between. According-ing to an etymological dictionary, moonlight streaming in through the closed doors suggests "at ease, sauntering, unoccupied, leisure." Thus the written images induce some such nuances—almost a feeling—to float across the Chinese imagination. Nor is this the end—from there the imagination takes off! An example is the character 意, *i*, meaning "thought, intention, inclination or purpose." A literal rendition of the combined pictogram might indicate the sound or voice of one's heart

Not only will a single Chinese character contain many different shades of meaning, but often a multitude of characters (or combinations of them) describes something expressed in English by one single unshaded word. Take daybreak, or dawn. In Chinese, a long list of pictures may be used for description from evocative ones such as 曉, *hsiao*, or the chattering of birds (characteristic of early morning) to two characters meaning before noon. Consider the pictures in the following short list.

旦　*tan*: dawn—the sun just above the horizon. (An early form of the character for sun was a simple picture. ⊙; for ease of writing and carving of wood-blocks this gradually developed into the modern form 日. The single horizontal line — represents the horizon.)

早　*tsao*: early morning, the start of the sun, or the sun a man-high.

晛　*hsien*: the sun just appearing, the first sight of the sun.

朝　*chao*: dawn—a boat and the sunrise, when men set out to fish.

平明 *p'in ming*: the dawn, the level light of dawn.

東　　*tung:* east, or sun rising; the sun shining through the trees

Wang Wei makes maximum use of the advantages inherent in his medium of expression. Each poem is like a stereoscopic image, one view filled with the feeling, the fragrance, the exquisite beauty of nature ; the other view, combined and superimposed, reflecting these moods in terms of human emotions. To Wang Wei nature was everywhere clothed with the supernatural. I believe that he was more deeply aware of the " Spirit in the woods " and its energy permeating every form of life than was even Wordsworth. This intuitive knowledge was part of his mystical heritage, intensified by his Taoist and Buddhist leanings. Many of his associates, many who belonged, as he did, to the literati, lived in constant reverence, if not actual worship, of nature. Weighted with religious significance, inscriptions were carved in the rocks of every mountain peak ; and in every wayside shrine surrounded by natural beauty, engraved tablets of stone were erected. Possessed of poetic as well as religious significance, they were a part of the expression of the rich cultural tradition of that time.

With a few exceptions, Wang Wei makes little attempt to tell stories in his poems. He seeks expression in tangible or concrete form in order that intimate and understanding companions may share his vision. Nor does Wang Wei often attempt to formulate philosophical truths. His approach to life's problems is very direct. His shorter poems are swift observations. Like breathing in and out, events and their repercussions upon his emotions succeed each other. As with most works of an intuitional character, he cares less about conveying meaning than in evoking psychic reactions.

Bamboo, by Wang Wei

Photograph of a rubbing taken from a stone tablet in the "Forest of Tablets," Sian, Shensi. Courtesy, Director of the Museum, Sian.

Translation of Inscription: There are two small paintings of bamboo by Wang Wei on the walls of the Court of the Eastern Pagoda in the K'ai-yüan Temple in Fêng-hsiang prefecture. These, with ink lines clearly visible, were discovered in 1068. Now, foolish and ignorant people are daily increasing and we are afraid that these pictures will vanish with drifting time and we shall lose the true meaning which the old Master meant to portray. Therefore we have obtained from Mr. Kuo copies which, made in 1056, are even better than the wall paintings. These we have had engraved on stone for those who are fond of these things. On the Winter Solstice, 1092, Yu Shih-hsiung of Wu Kung wrote: "Yü I-chih of Ch'ien Pei made the outlines for these engravings: Wang Cheng of Ping Yang wrote the Characters. Chi Hou-mu and Mêng Yung made the engravings."

Note: Although the dates of Wang Wei's life are frequently quoted as A. D. 699–759 (the dates recorded in the Old T'ang History), the New T'ang History gives the dates as A.D. 701–761. These are corroborated by Wang Wei's letter to Emperor Su-tsung thanking him for promoting his younger brother. Ref. *Wang Yu-ch'eng Chi Chien-chu*, Vol. 18, p. 4, Ssu-pu Pei-yao Edition.

THE LIFE OF WANG WEI

Although Wang Wei was also noted in his lifetime (A. D. 701–761) as a calligrapher, a musician and a medical practitioner, his fame throughout the ages rests upon two talents : his genius as a poet and his influence as a painter on succeeding generations. One common quotation about his work, " His poems are paintings, and his paintings, poems " is an accurate description of the way in which he identified these two major efforts of his life.

Wang Wei's achievements in poetry may justly rank with those of the " two great, " Tu Fu and Li Po. As an artist he is heralded for founding the Southern School of painting. This branch of the art was celebrated for a gentle, mystical quality, nevertheless thoroughly realistic. A legend demonstrating this realism has survived the centuries. Wang Wei is said to have painted a large rock for Prince Ch'i. One day in a storm a great gust of wind ripped the picture from its frame and blew it away. Shortly after, envoys from the King of Korea appeared bearing a real rock which, they said, had been deposited on Mount Shen-sun by a great gale ! Because it bore Wang Wei's seal it obviously belonged to the Emperor of China ; naturally, the King of Korea had not dared to keep it. A close comparison of that rock with those in Wang Wei's paintings convinced the Chinese Emperor that they were identical. Thereupon the rock was enshrined in the palace and to discourage its wandering spirit, the blood of a cock was poured over it. Nevertheless imagination was not lacking; Wang Wei at times did not hesitate to mix up his " four seasons, " placing a spring peach bloom with a late-flowering hibiscus, or a banana in snow!

Born in Ch'i, Shansi Province, of a father who was at one time Governor of Fên-chou, Wang Wei lived for sixty years in one of China's most illustrious periods of history. Hsüan Tsung who ascended the Dragon Throne in 713, gathered about him the most distinguished court that China, or the rest of the then-known world, had ever seen. Congregating at the capital Ch'ang-an, the City of Eternal Peace, were the finest intellects of China carefully winnowed by the most discriminating of examination systems. Here were assembled also the greatest artists of the land—painters, poets, musicians—men even now considered of first rank. It was one of those rare periods in history when some great creative force seems to lavish genius on a commonplace world. Furthermore, wise men from the West and from all the then civilized countries gathered at the court of China to drink of that unique inspiration, and to add some small sparkle to its brilliance.

According to the T'ang Dynasty Histories, Wang Wei began writing poetry as a precocious child of nine. Eight poems written in adolescence between the ages of fifteen and nineteen were always included in his mature

works.* When young he was vigorous, alert and ambitious, longing to achieve the glory of ancient heroes.
He wrote poems of worship to generals and warriors who
went to the frontier to fight against barbarians. He
also wrote poems admiring famous beauties of ancient
times**—for worshipping heroes and admiring beauties
is the natural bent of ambitious youths whether in the
East or West!

Since he was much interested in music, many of
Wang Wei's verses were written to be sung. When as
a young man of nineteen he went to the capital to take
his examination for the second degree it is said that his
musicianship more than his knowledge of literature was
responsible for his success. An accomplished player of
the p'i-p'a (the Chinese guitar), he was invited one spring
day by Prince Chi to the palace for dinner in honour of
the Princess. Many musicians were commanded to entertain the royal lady. Wang Wei presented her with
a new song, "Elegant Wheel Clock." Surprised and
delighted with his skill, the Princess ordered the exam-
iners to award Wang Wei first place as a candidate for
the second degree.

At the age of twenty-one, in a highly competitive
examination system, Wang Wei obtained the chin-shih
degree, roughly equivalent to the Western doctorate in
philosophy. This opened the door to officialdom in
China. He was appointed Director of Imperial Music.
But for some reason not known, he was subsequently

---

* Six of Wang Wei's early poems are included in this selection.
See poems 52, 101, 126, 128, 134, 136.
** See poems 41, 57, 58, 69, 126, 135. Also, poems 26, 27,
122, 134.

demoted and sent to be Keeper of the Granary in the small city of Chi-chou in Shantung Province. He expressed his disappointment in a poem.* With the fortitude of artists who cherish most the inner life, Wang Wei turned this seemingly barren period to advantage. He had time to read, rest and reflect; time to write some outstanding poetry.

In 734, when his friend Chang Chiu-ling (another famous poet) was made prime minister by Emperor Hsüan Tsung, he chose Wang Wei, then thirty-three years old, as Chief Advisor, and later as Imperial Censor. The duty of censor was to impeach officials for misbehaviour and to make remonstrance or suggest improvements concerning the acts of the Court. From that time on his official life proceeded smoothly. The same year his wife, of whom very little is known, died. He never remarried. His love for his mother seems to have exceeded even the deep filial respect which Chinese sons accord their parents. Upon her death in 742, he " cast off his official robes " and went home to mourn—so grievously that he became " like skin and bones " (as we still say today). After the " three-year " traditional mourning period for parents, he was again appointed Senior Secretary of the Board of Civil Service and later Imperial Secretary. This was the most prosperous period of his life. He became widely known as a poet; when he travelled with his brother to the national capitals princes and nobility entertained them in their own palaces, treating them with the reverence accorded teachers.

* See poem 109.

Wang Wei was devoted to his brother. When Wang Chin was absent from the capital as governor of Shuchou, Wang Wei presented a petition to the emperor saying that he, Wang Wei, had "five points of weakness" but his brother had "five points of strength;" therefore, he requested permission to retire as a farmer in order to let his brother return to the capital.

Not only was he deeply devoted to his family. His friends were legion. Nowhere in the world has friendship played so great a part and still does as in Chinese life. The old saying, "Never let principle interfere with friendship" expresses the depth of its influence. In many of his poems Wang Wei writes with warmth and spontaneity of his deep regard for his companions in poetry and religious faith. To P'ei Ti, in particular, he expresses his feeling of friendship with great sincerity :

We have not seen each other—
We have not seen each other for a long time.
At the source of the stream, day after day,
I recall how we used to clasp hands—
Hand in hand, eye to eye—because we had the same heart. . .
How I grieved when you left so unexpectedly!
That is the way I feel towards you even today—
This mutual love, then—is it deep? Or not !*

As Wang Wei grew older he tasted less of the sweet and more of the sour of life's flavour. His own burdens seemed to weigh so heavily on his heart as almost to overwhelm him. Financially he was actually well-off.

*See poem 129.

At one time as Minister of the Government he must have had ample security. Neverthless he frequently writes of himself as poor, lonely, forsaken and passed by.*

Real trouble did overtake him when, after capturing the two national capitals, Ch'ang-an and Lo-yang, the rebellious An Lu-shan, an adventurer of Mongol origin, forced Emperor Hsüan Tsung to flee to Chengtu, Szechwan. Wang Wei fell into the hands of enemy troops. In despair, he attempted to commit suicide with drugs. Failing in this, he then pretended to be dumb ! This did not help his situation. An Lu-shan, aware of Wang Wei's literary reputation and of his loyalty to the emperor, imprisoned him in the Temple of P'u-t'i in Lo-yang until the poet submitted to the only alternative offered—the position of an official in the usurping government.

Once, to entertain his officers in the Imperial Palace of Condensed Greenness,* An Lu-shan commanded the presence of many actors and musicians. While they were performing, many of them burst into tears. Wang Wei, when he learned of this incident, secretly protested in an indiscreet, rebellious poem. He little dreamed that this would help to save his own life For when the usurpers were eventually thrown out, not only were all officials who had served the enemy degraded three ranks but many were tried for treason. But Wang Wei's poem had become known all over the empire so he escaped censure. His brother, Wang Chin, Senior Secretary of the Board of Justice, interceded for him with the emperor and he was restored to his former official

* See poem 123, III. **See poem 65.

position. Two years before he died he was promoted to the position of Deputy-Minister in the Shang-shu Secretariat.

Honours, however, did not restore the poet's broken spirit. More and more he shut himself away from the outside world, finding as a recluse that elusive happiness no fame had brought him. He idealized the hermits; particularly those Seven Sages of the Bamboo Grove in the Six Dynasties who viewed the common people with contempt, "through the whites of their eyes." Now he devoted himself to the study of Buddhism. Entertaining as guests many famous Buddhist monks, he found deep contentment in religious discussions.

The beauty of nature had always been a passion with Wang Wei. Fortunately he managed to secure the home—Lan-t'ien Villa—of the famous poet, Sun Chih-wen. Encircled by mountains and the River Wang, from this base he and his friend P'ei Ti wandered endlessly. They composed poems together, or played their flutes, or drank wine, or strolled in the bright moonlight with their intimates, the Buddhist monks. No longer contending with the public, his life became absolutely tranquil. During an absence of his comrade (whom he seemed to hold in awe), Wang Wei wrote him a letter which best sums up the idyllic life of leisure of his last years :

"Of late, during the twelfth month, the weather has been clear and refreshing. I might have crossed the mountain to see you, but I thought that you would be reviewing the Classics so I felt that I did not dare disturb you. One day I walked alone on the mountain. I rested at the

Temple of Appreciation and dined with the monks. After dinner, I returned.

"*Going northward, I crossed the Yüan River over which the clear moon shone on the water with dazzling light. At night, I ascended Mount Hua-tzŭ and saw, far down below, the waves of the Wang River dancing up and down in the moonlight. Distant lights on the cold mountain glittered now and then beyond the forest. I could hear dogs barking in the deep lane. In the cold night they sounded like leopards! The beat of villagers pounding grain alternated with the toll of a monastery bell.*

"*Now the servants are quiet and I am sitting alone. I cannot help recalling our former days here together when we composed poems as we walked through narrow trails along the clear mountain streams.*

"*We must wait now for the coming of spring when grasses and trees will begin to grow luxuriously once more. Then we shall be able to roam again in these spring hills and see the trout leap lightly out of the water, and watch the white gulls fly back and forth. Heavy dew will water the green ground and pheasants will crow in the wheat-fields in the early dawn . . . It will not be long. Do come and wander about with me then!*

"*If I did not know your subtly natural talents I would not dare send you such an unnecessary invitation. But there is a deep interest for me in what I have done. So, I am asking a woodsman to take you this letter.*

"*With respect: written by*

Wang Wei,
(A dweller in the mountains . . .)"

POEMS OF FOUR FIVE-CHARACTER LINES

Twenty Poems of Wang-ch'uan Valley
1-20

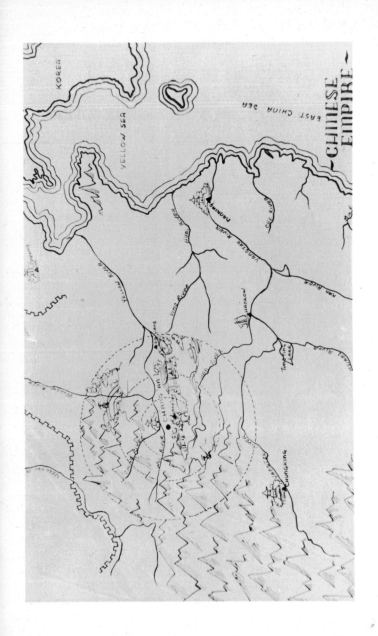

FOREWORD
by
WANG WEI

My cottage was in the Wang-ch'uan Valley. My
wanderings included many places : Mêng-ch'êng Valley,
Mount Hua-tzŭ, My Study Among Beautiful Apricot
Trees, A Hill of Graceful Bamboo, Deer Forest Her-
mitage, Magnolia Hermitage, Rivers of Dogwood, A
Path through Imperial Locust Trees, An Arbour beside
the Lake, South Hill, Beside Lake Yi, Waves of
Willow, At the Rapids of the Luan Family, The Stream
of Powdered Gold, White Stone Bank, North Hill, My
Hermitage in the Bamboo Grove, Hibiscus Hill, The
Lacquer Tree Garden, and The Pepper Tree Garden.
During that period, my good friend P'ei Ti and I com-
posed poems at leisure.

The river Wang-ch'uan, with head waters at the entrance to
Mount Chiang, flows south of Lan-t'ien, Shensi Province, through
a deep valley into a large pool. Except for one narrow path,
Mount Chiang abounds in precipices so no other passage can
be followed. Several miles south, the mountains dwindle into a
wide-open plain from which, looking back, one sees only the
crowding peaks. Still further south are thirteen places noted
for beautiful scenery ; among them the temple of Deer Forest
that became Wang Wei's villa.

1. MÊNG-CH'ÊNG VALLEY

My new home stands sentinel at the entrance to
    Mêng-ch'êng
Where, of an ancient wood, only time-worn willows
    still remain . . .
Who would come to live in this lonely place
Unless to brood over the sorrows of the past?

2. MOUNT HUA-TZǓ

Birds sail endlessly across the sky.
Again the mountain range wears autumn's hue.
As I wander up and down Mount Hua-tzǔ
Deep shafts of sorrow pierce me!

3. MY STUDY AMONG BEAUTIFUL APRICOT TREES

Slender apricot trees pillar my hermitage,
Fragrant grasses thatch it;
Mountain clouds drift through it—
Clouds, could you not better make rain for
    needy peasants?

4. A HILL OF GRACEFUL BAMBOO

Sandalwoods cast shadows across empty trails.
Dark blue ripples race on the river.
Secretly I enter the pathway to Mount Shang;
Not even the woodcutter knows I am here.

5. DEER FOREST HERMITAGE

Through the deep wood, the slanting sunlight
Casts motley patterns on the jade-green mosses.
No glimpse of man in this lonely mountain,
Yet faint voices drift on the air.

6. MAGNOLIA HERMITAGE

The autumn hills hoard scarlet from the setting sun.
Flying birds chase their mates,
Now and then patches of blue sky break clear . . .
Tonight the evening mists find nowhere to gather.

7. RIVERS OF DOGWOOD

Green dogwood berries ripen to crimson
Though blossoms still star the branches.
Come friends !   How can you bear not to stay
   in these mountains
And savour that rich red wine with me !

8. A PATH THROUGH IMPERIAL
LOCUST TREES

The narrow path hides beneath imperial locust trees ;
Thick green mosses carpet the shaded earth.
While sweeping the courtyard, I keep watching the gate
Lest my friend, the mountain monk, should visit me.

9. IN AN ARBOUR BESIDE THE LAKE

My light skiff, garnished to welcome esteemed guests,
Leisurely floats along the lake.
On the shaded balcony we sit with our wine-cups
Mid lotus blossoms blooming in four directions

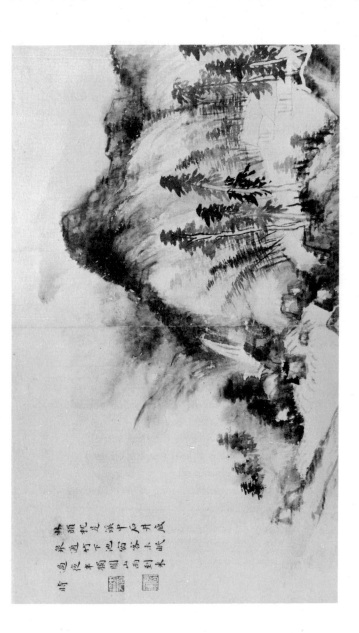

10. SOUTH HILL

A small boat sails to South Hill;
North Hill is hard to reach—the river is wide.
On the far shore I see families moving,
Too distant to be recognized.

11. BESIDE LAKE YI

Where the lake ends, she sits now playing her flute.
At dusk she bade farewell to her husband.
Wistfully she stares across the water,
Watching a white cloud rolling up the blue mountain
    side.

12. WAVES OF WILLOW

The swaying branches of the willow row mingle their
    silken garments in caresses.
Reflected shadows ripple the clear water.
Be not like those willows weeping on the
    imperial embankment
Which sadden people parting in the cold spring wind . . .

The long slender willow branch was symbolic of the thread of
longing which bound intimate friends together. In the T'ang
Dynasty (A. D. 618-907) the custom of snapping twigs along
the imperial embankment represented parting.

13. AT THE RAPIDS OF THE LUAN FAMILY

Under the spatter of October rain
The shallow water slides over slippery stones;
Leaping waves strike each other
And frightened, the egret dares not dive for fish.

14. THE STREAM OF POWDERED GOLD

He who drinks daily from the Stream of Powdered Gold
Shall live at least a thousand years!
Then he will be presented to the Jade Emperor,
Riding beneath a plumed canopy in a carriage drawn by
    soaring blue phoenixes and spirited young dragons.

The Jade Emperor, Yü Huang, was the Taoist Supreme Lord
of the physical world and saviour of man.

15. WHITE STONE BANK

White Stone Bank River, shallow, clear,
Meanders past a sparse handful of rushes.
Families on the east and west banks
Wash silk in the silver moonlight.

16. NORTH HILL

North Hill stands out above the lake
Against thick evergreens gleams startlingly
   a vermilion gate.
Below, South River zig-zags toward the horizon,
Glistening, here and there, beyond the tree-tops of the
   blue forest.

17. MY HERMITAGE IN THE
BAMBOO GROVE

Deep in the bamboo grove, sitting alone,
I thrum my lute as I whistle a tune.
No one knows I am in this thicket
Save the bright moon looking down on me.

18. HIBISCUS HILL

The blossoms on high hibiscus boughs
Fling crimson through the mountains.
Families no longer live in this deserted valley,
Yet season after season the hibiscus still blooms in
   profusion.

19. THE LACQUER TREE GARDEN

The keeper of the Lacquer Tree Garden was no
   proud official:
That old sage knew nothing of worldly matters.
When by chance, he received this low-ranking office,
He sauntered about lazily caring for a few
   gnarled trees !

Chuang Tzŭ, the great philosopher and follower of Laotzŭ, was
keeper of the Lacquer Tree Garden at one time.

20. THE PEPPER TREE GARDEN

With a flask of cinnamon wine, we welcome the
   daughters of Emperor Yao;
To the Beautiful Goddess, we present fragrant grasses
And we greet the Prince of the Clouds
With a peppery drink and delectable feast.

Based on a legend of the Warring States Period (B. C. 481-221)
when the speaker, Ch'ü Yüan was a famous poet. The daughters of Emperor Yao after their death became fairies. The
Beautiful Goddess and Prince of the Clouds ; also fairies.

POEMS OF FOUR FIVE-CHARACTER LINES

Miscellaneous Poems
21-46

21. PARTING

I watch you travel slowly down the mountain
And then the sun is gone.   I close my thatched door.
Grasses will grow green again next spring;
But you, beloved friend, will you return?

22. LONGING FOR LOVE

Love seeds grow in the South
Budding in spring on every bough.
My friend, gather them recklessly!
They bring me love's fondest memories.

The red seeds of *Abrus precatorius*, used for love potions, are
known as "love seeds" or seeds for the "mutually lovesick."
Lovers exchange them to express their longing for each other.

23. ASCENDING THE TERRACE TO WATCH ADVISOR LI DEPART

I climb the lofty terrace to see you off;
The river and mountains fade into infinity
And weary birds turn homeward in blue dusk;
Only the traveller walks on and on, unresting.

24. *LEAVING WANG-CH'UAN COTTAGE*

Sadly, with deep longing to stay on, I drive my carriage
Out of the pine trees twisted with vines . . .
I must endure the sorrow of leaving these
    green mountains,
But can I forget their blue streams?

25. *AN ORAL POEM COMPOSED ON HORSE-BACK TO BID GOOD-BYE TO NINTH BROTHER TSUI WHO IS LEAVING FOR SOUTH MOUNTAIN*

Here we are at the corner of the city wall, about to part.
When shall we meet again!
Count the days by the cassia flowers in those
    southern hills
And do not wait until their petals fall like snow.

26. *MADAME HSI*

In spite of today's Imperial Grace,
She cannot forget the kindness of yesteryear's husband.
Full of tears, she fixes her gaze on flowers,
And will not speak to the King of Ch'u.

27. MADAME PAN CHIEH-YÜ

I

Shadows of fireflies flit across her jade window,
Men's voices vanished from the golden palace.
She huddles behind the lattice these fall evenings—
Her lonely light burns brightly—then goes out.

II

Autumn grass grows tall in the palace court
But the Emperor's favour grows short.
How can she bear to listen to sweet music!
His golden chariot no longer pauses outside her
    chamber.

III

Her dressing room is closed—small wonder.
After the morning levee she welcomes him no more.
When she walks in her spring garden
Mocking whispers blended with laughter rise among the
    flowers.

28. POEM ON A FRIEND'S MARBLE SCREEN

On that screen of natural marble in your home
Facing the open courtyard,
Mountain springs flow as fresh as in nature.
Yet they are not even painted.

Chinese craftsmen take great pleasure in polishing the coloured
strata in marble slabs to bring out landscape effects.

Detail of *Mountain Scenery with Monk*,
by Huang Chun-pi, Contemporary Artist
Collection of L.C. Walmsley
See poem 32

29. RED PEONIES

Patiently the peonies mature cupped by ripe green leaves,
Robed in all crimson shades from light to dark.
Their hearts must be ready to break—the seasons pass
    so soon.
Can radiant Spring understand their feelings?

30. TWO SONGS OF SPRING WANDERING

I

Ten thousand apricots bordering the river bank
Burst into bloom by a single night of spring wind;
Rioting with colours light and dark,
The entire orchard floats on the blue river ripples.

II

In the upper garden there is no end of trees.
Each morning new blossoms appear.
Below pass fragrant carts drawn by decorated horses
Puffing up dust without even a breeze.

31. PEAR FLOWERS LEFT OF
THE PALACE

Beyond the bamboo screen, petals flutter lightly in the
    breeze
Scattered in drifts across the grass beside the
    marble steps . . .
Ah, more than the song of the nightingale
Disturbs the hearts of young girls in the
    Palace of Wei-yang.

32. ANOTHER POEM COMPOSED ORALLY TO P'EI TI

How can I escape from the entanglements of life?
I shall shake off the official robes and withdraw from
    this noisy world!
Taking my goosefoot staff
I shall leisurely travel to Peach Blossom Spring.

T'ao Ch'ien (A. D. 372-427) wrote an essay about the happy
life of people who avoided the chaos of the Ch'in Dynasty by
going to live in a fairy-land, the Peach Blossom Spring. See, "A
Song of Peach Blossom River," poem 136.

33. THREE POEMS

I

The cottage where I now live
Faces the outlet of Mêng-chin River.
Boats come often from the south
Will they, I wonder, take my letters home?

II

You have come from my native village.
You must know what is happening there?
The day you left—did you notice that winter plum
By my latticed window? Was it yet in bloom?

III

Already blossoms climb the winter plum here,
And bird song is heard once more.
With a sad heart I note the spring grass turning green
    yet again:
I fear lest it over-grow the marble stairs.

34. A PORTRAIT OF TS'UI HSING-TSUNG

I painted your portrait when your years were young;
Now I have painted you when you are old
Yet in this picture I discover a new man!
I understood you better in the old days ...

35. MOUNTAIN DOGWOOD

Red dogwood blooming at the foot of the mountain
Heavily scents the cool air with pungent fragrance ...
At least I have clusters of cassia flowers
Blooming beside my window which faces the
    harvest moon.

36. WEEPING OVER THE DEATH OF
MÊNG HAO-JAN

I shall never see my old friend again ...
Day after day the Han River flows onward to the sea.
Oh, elders of Hsiang-yang,
Do the hills and waters of Ts'ai-chou keep silence now?

Ts'ai-chou was Mêng Hao-jan's native place.

37. *IN THE MOUNTAIN*

White pebbles jut out from the Ching River.
Few red leaves remain in the cold weather.
Though no rain soaks these mountain paths,
Green mists moisten the traveller's clothing.

The Ching River flows by the town of Lan-t'ien.

38. *A SONG ON PARTING WITH SPRING*

Day after day we can't help growing older.
Year after year spring can't help seeming younger.
Come let's enjoy our winecup today,
Not pity the flowers fallen!

39. *WRITTEN IMPRESSIONS*

The shaded tower is spattered with dewdrops of rain.
During the day, the great court-yard remains closed.
As I gaze steadily at blue mosses about me,
Their colour seems to creep up my blue gown!

Drawing, by Lo Po-chin, Contemporary Artist
Contemporary Collection of Chang Yin-nan
See poem 42

TRANSLATION OF COLOPHON

Gradually the clouds and fog cover the sky ;
An old man sits alone in his pavilion by the river.
He is not worried by the rushing wind and the rain,
But he is concerned that his friends are late in coming.

I

As he leaves for his garrison far away, this proud
    young man
Draws his precious knife from its scabbard with a clang!
His hour has struck to repay the Imperial Favour.
Today he thinks lightly of his life.

II

The barbarians along the frontier are ever at war with us.
Already the border wind has blown in the
    coming of autumn.
Our hero, always by temperament ambitious,
Through skill as an archer will achieve the
    title of marquis.

41. *TRAVELLING ALONG THE FRONTIER*

With feathered arrows slung across his back, he reaches
    the border of his district.
Playing his reed flute, he marches across the frontier.
Yellow clouds warn him that the fort is not far now . . .
Withered grasses whisper the arrival of fall.

42. REPLYING TO P'EI TI

How cold and wide the mighty waters flow!
November rain darkens the day.
Do you ask where Chung-nan is hidden?
My heart answers, "There it lies, beyond those
    white clouds!"

Mount Chung-nan, thought by Chinese poets to be a place for
hermits and immortals.

43. A POEM TO MY BROTHERS AND SISTERS WRITTEN FROM THE MOUNTAIN

Hidden on this mountain, many Buddhist monks
Chant sutras, meditate together;
Men on distant city walls gazing towards the peaks
See only white, enshrouding clouds.

44. FROM A MAID TO HER FARAWAY LOVER—FIVE POEMS

I

Spring! Bright flowers gaily dance along the pathway;
Old weeping willows, newly wrapped in tender green,
    gently brush the imperial embankment.
Remind my wayward lover in Liao-yang
How flowing time will never wait for man!

Liao-yang: a county in Manchuria.

Monastery among the Mists, by Sun K'o-hung. 1532—1610
Courtesy, C.T. Loo, New York
See poem 43

II

Drafted while still of low rank, he was sent far away.
She grieves in her lonely chamber, feeling old and ugly.
Though bravely she puts on her finest silks to match
the spring-clad trees,
Her tears run silently together in strings of a
thousand pearls.

III

Nightingales sing in the dense green leaves;
Swallows twitter in the dusk on the carved ridgebeams.
Since he walked through her door, not one single word!
How far has he marched toward the battle-front?

IV

So sudden our parting—cutting form from shadow!
Now a thousand miles of misty waves divide us.
If you search for our trysting place, alas!
You will only find white clouds rising.

V

Tonight's moon shimmers on the women's chambers
Like silk—but cold as hoar frost—
Shining indifferently on lovers who, grieved at parting,
Lie sleepless till the lonely gray of dawn ...

45. WHILE LISTENING TO P'EI TI HUMMING POETRY, I COMPOSE A POEM TO HIM IN FUN

How bitter the wail of the monkeys
Mourning from daylight till dark!
Come now!   Do not ape their cries in the
   Wu Gorge
Lest you break the hearts of travellers on the
   autumn river!

Wu Gorge: famous gorge in the upper Yangtze River.

46. TO WEI MU, THE EIGHTEENTH

We hermits understand each other;
We both have white-cloud hearts.
Why need we withdraw to East Mountain to contemplate
When right here we never lift a finger, even to keep
   spring grass from growing rank!

White-cloud hearts: symbolizing the peace of mountain hermits.
The last line of this poem suggests the place is so secluded
that the young grass is untrodden by visitors.

POEMS OF FOUR FIVE-CHARACTER LINES

Five Poems on a River with Clouds Along the Huang-Fu Range
47-51

47.   THE SONG-OF-BIRDS STREAM

Idly I watch the cassia petals gently fall.
How still the night !   Blue mountains loom
   stark and lonely.
The low-hung moon grows brilliant, startling the
   wild birds
To doleful cries echoing through the dark valley.

48.   LOTUS FLOWER EMBANKMENT

Day after day you go gathering lotus blossoms,
Returning each late dusk from the long island . . .
Be careful, playing with that boat pole,
Lest you dampen your garment embroidered with red
   lotus blooms !

49.   EGRET DYKE

Swoop !   The egret dives into the red lotus blossoms.
Splash !   He breaks the clear water into waves.
How handsome he looks in his new-born feathered silk
Proudly balanced on the old raft, a fish in his beak . . .

50. RICE FIELDS

Farmers till their rice paddies at break of day
Toiling, tilling late into the night.
Ask the man who would seek of them the Way
If he has heard of the virtuous hermits Chü and Ni.

Ch'ang Chü and Chieh Ni   Hermits of the Ch'un Ch'iu Period
B. C. 770–480.   Confucius, lost once, asked his disciple Tzŭ-lu
to seek direction from these two sages.   They took this oppor-
tunity to lecture Confucius on life.   See *Analects*: 18 : 6.

51. DUCKWEED POND

Broad and deep lies the pond in spring.
I wait to meet the light skiff returning;
Green duckweed closes in the wake of the boat—
Then the weeping willow brushes it wide apart
    once more.

POEMS OF FOUR
SEVEN-CHARACTER
LINES

52-76

52. ON THE NINTH-DAY-OF-THE-NINTH-MOON FESTIVAL I LONG TO SEE MY BROTHERS

I am a stranger in a strange land.
On every annual festival, I doubly long for my
homefolk.
I think of my far-away brothers climbing the mountains ;
Surely they will miss me when they pin on
sprigs of dogwood !

Festival of the Ninth-Day-of-the-Ninth-Moon : the Festival of
Ascending High Mountains. Sprigs of dogwood were supposed
to drive away evil spirits.

53. TWO SONGS OF AUTUMN LONGING

I

The cold breeze blows through the pearl-curtained
chamber, stirring my thin garments.
I hear faintly in the depths of night, the drop, drop,
drop, of the jade water-clock.
The moon has ferried the Heavenly River ; mists of
morning pale her waning light.
Roused from sleep, birds flutter the leaves in the trees.

Heavenly River: the Milky Way.

On the Pool of Sublimity near the palace, white ruffles
the blue water.

Gradually summer heat fades and tang of autumn shar-
pens the air

During the night a light breeze tips up the leaves of the
duckweed

And all across the pond, dew-pearls flutter and whirl on
the lotus leaves.

54. *TWO SONGS OF AN AUTUMN NIGHT*

I

While the water-clock drops—ting—ting, how
long the night!

The moonlight sifts across the earth through
scudding clouds.

In the still cool of autumn, the insects' cry persists
through the long darkness . . .

Frost, please stay away! The winter clothing is yet to
be sent to the front.

II

Newly born, the crescent moon; pale, the
autumn mist . . .

She has not yet changed her silk garments, already far
too thin;

Feverishly she plays her silver harp all through the
night,

Her heart too full of fear to return to
her empty chamber.

55. *A SONG OF THE CITY OF WEI*

A morning rain has settled the light dust in the city of
  Wei,
And slaked the thirst of green willows framing the
  guest house.
Come, my comrades, drink with me one more
  cup of wine—
West of the frontier you will meet no more old friends.

56. *TO TUAN, THE SIXTEENTH*

The first time I met you we became fast friends.
Having heard that your house stood beside the
  River Mêng,
Now, when boats come sailing by, I always ask
If anyone from Lo-yang is on board.

57. *FOUR POEMS TO BRAVE YOUTHS*

I

Ten thousand flasks of Hsin-fêng's aged wine
Must have gone down the gullets of Hsien-yang's
  young gallants.
Their horses hitched to the willows weeping beside the
  tavern,
How boisterously these revelling comrades would toast
  each other's health!

II

He starts by becoming an officer in the
    Imperial bodyguard;
His first command, to follow General Ho fighting in
    Yü-yang.
Everyone knows that life on the frontier is bitter—
Still, if he dies, his chivalrous bones will be fragrant!

III

Alone, he can draw two carved bows at once!
A thousand waves of enemy horsemen cannot daunt him.
Astride his golden saddle, he strings his bow with white-
    feathered arrows,
And ping! the plumed shower drops five khan dead!

IV

After a delectable feast in the Han Court,
The Emperor with his officers returns to the Cloud
    Terrace, and in council earnestly discusses the
    war awards.
Then proceeding to the balcony, bestows upon the
    general the seal of marquis.
Thus proudly adorned, the new nobleman struts out of
    the Palace of Great Brightness.

58. TO GENERAL P'EI MIN

Seven stars flash brightly on the sword at your side;
On your arm, the carved bow flaunts honours from a
hundred battles.
Still, not until rumours flew of the capture of the Yün-
chung barbarians,
Did it dawn upon us—a general graces our imperial
court!

59. LIGHT VERSE ON WANG-CH'UAN COTTAGE

The willow branches bow so low we need not pluck
them, token of farewell;
The pine trees pierce the clouds—as the eye climbs
them their crests seem heaven-high!
The purple wistaria, tangled with shadows, could hide
even a yellow-haired monkey
And on the lush cypress, musk deer could grow fat.

60. LIGHT VERSE ON A ROCK

I pity the inert rock by the flowing stream
And the willows trailing fingers into my wine-cup . . .
But who can say the spring wind is not aware of the
sound in my heart?
Why else should it blow these frail falling petals
about me?

61. WITH OFFICIAL LU HSIANG, PASSING HERMIT TS'UI HSIN-CHUNG'S BOWER

Green forests cover the four directions with dense
    deep shade.
Every day untrodden mosses cushion the courtyard more
    thickly in bluish gray.
Under tall pines the hermit sprawls, legs outstretched,
Turning upon the vulgar crowd only the whites of
    his eyes.

In the Chin Dynasty (A. D. 265-419) there was a band of
Taoists known as the "Seven Sages of the Bamboo Grove"
who would converse only with the intelligent. When they met
the "vulgar" they looked at them in contempt only through
"the whites of their eyes."

62. FAREWELL

As I see you off at the South Bank, my tears run into
    silken threads.
Your leaving for an eastern country gives me a
    sick heart.
I grieve at the news of my old friends—scattered,
    dying—
How different, these days, from the golden age at Lo-
    yang!

63. FAREWELL TO SHEN TZÛ-FU WHO IS TRAVELLING EAST OF THE YANGTZE RIVER

Few voyagers gather at the ferry beneath the willows.
Plying his oar, the boatman zig-zags along the river bank.
I am left alone with my longing, the nostalgic colour of springtime ;
Be you north or south of the Yangtze, ever with yearning I follow your homeward way.

64. COMPOSED ON THE HAN-SHIH FESTIVAL AT THE SZÛ RIVER

As the traveller from Wen-yang returns homeward, he meets the late spring near the city of Kuang-wu.
Tears moisten his handkerchief . . .
Petals fall quietly ; birds call in the mountains.
Beneath an arch of fresh green willows the ferryman crosses the river.

On Han-shih (festival without fire), a spring festival, people ate only cold food.

65. TO P'EI TI

I am broken hearted : ten thousand families lost, turned
    into wild smoke !
When again will the hundred officers wait upon the
    Emperor ?
Leaves from the locust trees litter the courts of the
    deserted palace . . .
Yet listen ! From the end of the Pool of Condensed
    Greenness come faint sounds of merry music.

Wang Wei is lamenting the ill fortune of his emperor. The
royal palaces were occupied by the followers of the rebel leader,
An Lu-shan.

66. WEEPING OVER YIN YAO'S DEATH

After your burial on Stone-tower Mountain,
The mourners in their chariots wind downward through
    dark pines and cypresses.
Your bones interred beneath the white clouds, your life
    forever ended ;
Only the flowing stream lives on in the world of men.

67. SIGHING OVER MY WHITE HAIR

Youth's ruddy cheeks so soon sink in on fallen teeth
And childhood's hanging locks so swifty turn to snow.
In a single lifetime, how many happenings
    break the heart !
If I cannot enter a monastery, where else can I
    bury my sorrow ?

68. TWO SONGS OF SPRING WANDERING

I

The silken willow wands arching the loitering river,
    unfold into smoky strings of leaves;
The ice in the cold ravine melts in the warm air.
When the glory of spring has been born again along
    these flower-laden paths,
We shall already have heard people playing gay tunes
    from the inspiring Yün and Shao.

II

Wandering along the willow-bordered trail and over
    Peach Blossom Stream,
Hungering for the brightness of spring—everywhere
    beauty enchants me !
Flying birds dart now and then to scatter the
    willow catkins ;
Boughs, overburdened, bend beneath whorls of blossoms.

Yün and Shao : ritual music dating back to the legendary period
of the Yellow Emperor, B. C. 2698–2598?, and Emperor Shun,
B. C. 2255–2205.

69. TWO SONGS ON CONQUERING THE TARTARS

I

High in the autumn sky, the Great White Star aids the
    troops of Han ;
Few barbarians remain.   The fierce winds fall at night.
Throwing off their swords young soldiers,
Happy once more, enjoy the peace of kingly rule.

The Great White Star : the evening star, Venus.

The wind tugs the flapping flags ; a new spirit of cheer-
fulness pervades his men.

So quickly he obeyed the Imperial command to settle
the dust of the barbarians,

That his portrait now hangs in the Tower of the Uni-
corn at the Imperial Palace

And today he ranks first in all the court !

70. A MAIDEN'S LONGING FOR SPRING

With heavy grief she watches a thousand-foot gossamer
web floating in the breeze

Only to be battered and broken by the spring wind
even as her longing heart by separation.

With no one can she share her sorrow through the long
lonely day . . .

Petals drop quietly on the green moss.

71. TWO POEMS TO BE SENT FAR AWAY

I

This year I am living alone in an empty room ;

In my dreams I see the mountain passes over which so
often you have left me ;

No wild goose runs to me with your letters . . .

Forlorn, I watch the new moon shaped like the eyebrow
of a moth.

The wild goose : a symbol for the postal service. A story from
the Han Dynasty, (B. C. 206- A. D. 220) tells of Su Wu, who
when captured by tribesmen, tied a letter to the foot of a wild
goose to send a message back to his emperor, Han Wu Ti.

II

Weary of plucking willow twigs by the green tower—
Idly, I gather lotus blossoms beside the blue pool.
I ride my horse to the edge of the terrace, but not a
  sign of my man . . .
A fierce battle must be starting on the Mound
  Brushed by Clouds.

72. POEM WITHOUT A TITLE

Bitterly I long for you in this fresh breeze and
  clear moonlight,
Vagrant, lost to me in the army more than ten years!
Did I not especially beseech you, warrior, the day you
  left me
To send back letters as often as the wild goose returned?

73. FOLLOWING THE ARMY

When the star Mao T'ao fell into darkness, the message
  —victory—was quickly despatched.
Now at the Golden Gate the runners await their reward,
  official robes.
This general astride his white horse always
  defeats his enemy . . .
But when will the drafted soldiers fighting at the Yellow
  Dragon return?

According to legend when the star Mao T'ao fell there would
be a barbarian uprising.

74. IN DOUBT ABOUT A DREAM

Be not disquieted either by kindness or by insult—
empty joy or sorrow.
Do not count on good or evil—you will only waste
your time . . .
And why seek advice from the Yellow Emperor or
Confucius?
Who knows but that we all live out our lives in the
maze of a dream?

75. A FAREWELL TO HSIN CHIEN IN THE HIBISCUS TOWER

Last night you came to the kingdom of Wu; a cold
rain covered the river.
This morning, in the level light of dawn, I must bid
you farewell as you travel through the lonely Ch'u
mountains.
If in Lo-yang, my friends and home folk ask about me,
Tell them my far-away heart is a splinter of ice in a
jade jug!

Wu was in the present Kiangsu-Chekiang area; Ch'u, in Honan-
Hupeh district.

76. THANKING THE SPIRIT OF
LIANG-CHOU

Few travel beyond the city wall of Liang-chou.

From the crest of a hundred-foot mound I gaze out
across the frontier regions

Where valiant soldiers beat on drums and play their
shepherd flutes.

They are competing at the east of the city to render
thanks to the God of the Horsemen.

POEMS OF FOUR SIX-CHARACTER
LINES

77

77. JOYS OF COUNTRY LIFE
SEVEN POEMS

I

Travelling to northern hamlets or southern villages
People pass in and out through a thousand gates and
    ten thousand houses.
How senseless riding back and forth on horses adorned
    with tinkling jades!
Who was that man from Mount K'ung-t'ung with dis-
    hevelled hair, important enough to be asked about
    Tao by the Yellow Emperor?

The legendary Yellow Emperor when on K'ung-t'ung mountain,
Honan, enquired of the Way (Tao) from Kuang Ch'êng-tzü, one
of the Immortals.

II

In his first conversation with the king of Chao, the
    hermit Yü Ch'ing was rewarded with a pair of
    white jades;
On his second visit he had conferred upon him a
    dukedom of ten thousand families.
Is he better than the peasant cultivating his
    southern field?
Then why should he not sleep high behind an
    eastern window?

When Yü Ch'ing, a hermit in the Warring States, B. C. 481-
221, first visited the king of Chao he was presented with two
pieces of white jade and one hundred taels of gold. On the
second, he was appointed a high ranking officer. The third
time he received the ensign of premier with the title of duke.
"Sleep high behind an eastern window:" become a hermit.

III

Breasting the fierce wind, some gather water chestnuts
at the end of the ferry landing;
Others, leaning on staffs, stroll about the village to the
west in the slanting sun.
A fisherman lingers on the Terrace of Apricots.
All are hermits who live like the fairies in Peach
Blossom River.

IV

Clusters of fragrant grass turn green with the spring;
In summer, tall pines scatter coolness.
Cows and sheep unattended wind homeward along nar-
row village lanes . .
Untutored urchins do not even recognize a scholar when
they see one!

V

At the foot of the mountain, solitary smoke curls upward
from a distant village;
On a high plateau, a lonely tree brushes the very
edge of Eternity.
Down a little pathway lives a Mr. Yen Hui;
In a door opposite, a Mr. Five Willows.

According to Chuang Tzŭ, Confucius used to teach his dis-
ciples on the Terrace of Apricots. Once a hermit fisherman
came to the terrace and listened to Confucius with great respect.
Yen Hui: a favourite disciple of Confucius. Mr. Five Willows
refers to T'ao Ch'ien, A. D., 365-427, a famous poet. He
planted five willow trees in front of his house.

VI

The pink peach blossoms still hoard night rain;
Green willows grow greener still misted with spring.
Petals keep falling—more for the gardener to sweep!
The golden orioles sing—how can the mountain guest
    sleep on and on!

VII

The men always gather by the stream when they
    drink wine;
Leaning against the tall pines, they strum their lutes.
They pluck their sunflowers in the southern garden in
    the early morning,
And late in the evening they beat out their yellow
    grain in the eastern valley.

POEMS OF EIGHT
FIVE-CHARACTER LINES

78-111

78 TO SCHOLAR P'EI TI, FROM ONE WHO LIVES LEISURELY IN A COTTAGE AT WANG-CH'UAN

The shivering mountains turn to indigo;
The autumn stream flows murmuring all day long.
Beyond my covered gate, I lean upon my staff
And listen to the wind-borne cry of the dying cicada.
Descending, the sun loiters over the ferry-landing
And lonely smoke lingers above the sleepy village . . .
Again I meet you, drunken modern hermit Chieh Yü,
Madly serenading Five Willows Cottage!

Chieh Yü: an ancient hermit, famous for having halted Confucius with this song:
> O phoenix, O phoenix,
> How corrupt virtue is!
> The past cannot be admonished,
> But the future may be pursued,
> Be away, be away—
> The present politics are dangerous'

79. REPLYING TO OFFICIAL SU WHO VISITED LAN-T'IEN VILLA, ONLY TO FIND NO ONE AT HOME

I live humbly beside a mountain pass.
Tall trees encircle the deserted village . . .
Alas! To think you wasted your time travelling back
  and forth over this stony path!
When again will anyone wait before my door?
My fishing boat is iced fast in the frozen river;
And below on the frigid plain a hunter's fire burns.
Beyond bank up white clouds . . .
I hear only the faint tolling of a bell and the eerie cry
  of monkeys in the night.

80. RETURNING TO MOUNT SUNG

How clear the river, girdled by tail shrubs,
Flowing and singing in sympathy with my thoughts.
Leisurely my horse-cart moves along.
Evening birds accompany me on my homeward way . . .
Overlooking the old ferry sleeps the deserted city.
Flames of sunset fire the whole autumnal mountain.
How far I have travelled to reach the
    foot of Mount Sung !
Home at last, let me close my door and shut out the
    noisy world.

81. AN ANSWER TO ASSISTANT
MAGISTRATE CHANG

In the sunset years of my life, all I desire is quietude ;
The ten thousand affairs of this world no longer involve
    my heart.
As to my future ?   I have no better plan
Than to retreat to my old forest.
There the pine wind will loosen my girdle
And the mountain moon will smile on me as I
    pluck my lute.
Sir, do you ask the principle behind success and failure?
Listen to the fisherman's song drifting up from the deep
    river estuary.

82. CHUNG-NAN RANGE

T'ai-yi rising heavenward near the imperial capital,
Joins the vast range rolling down to a corner of the sea.
As I look back, white clouds close-gather ;
Yet once within the mountains, the blue mists vanish.
One central rampart divides the wilderness into
    many folds ;
Shadow and sunshine race across the valleys.
Sould I need a night's lodging,
I have only to ask the woodcutter over the river.

T'ai-yi : a famous peak in Chung-nan Range.

83. ON PASSING THE MONASTERY OF ACCUMULATED FRAGRANCE

Ignorant of the way to the Monastery of Accumulated
    Fragrance,
I wandered many miles through cloud-caught peaks
And ancient forests, spying no trace of human footstep.
Whence then, the faint peal of a temple bell ?
A gurgling stream chokes on treacherous rocks ;
The dying sun flicks coldly through the blue pines.
By a quiet pool designed for meditation
I subdue the Poisonous Dragon, passion.

84. LOOKING ACROSS THE COUNTRYSIDE ON A FINE NEW DAY

The plain stretches farther on this fresh, bright morning,
Far as the eye can see—and dustless.
The city gate stands guard beside the ferry,
Village trees tunnel the river to the end ;
White water gleams in the distant paddies
And blue peaks rear beyond the foothills.
During the farming season not one soul is idle,
The entire family clan works the southern fields.

85. COMPOSED ON A SPRING DAY ON THE FARM

Spring pigeons bill and coo under the roofs ;
Returning swallows spy out their former nests ;
Apricot blossoms whiten the outskirts of the village.
Axes in hand, the peasants set out to prune the
    mulberry trees,
Or shouldering hoes, explore water sources for irrigation.
Old people leaf over the latest almanac.
As for me, with my cup of wine, I suddenly
    forget to drink,
Whelmed in abysmal longing for friends far away.

86. A FAREWELL TO OFFICIAL LIU
LEAVING FOR AN-HSI

A wilderness of Tartar sand overlaid with frontier dust
Stretches across the Yang Pass to that remote country.
Wild geese fly the empty skies during three brief
  months of spring;
Within ten thousand miles how few the travellers!
Yet over the same torturous route alfalfa followed the
  " heavenly horses;"
And strange grapes from the city of Han.
Come, let us freeze these barbarians with fear of
  our forces
So they dare not make peace by marrying our princesses!

The " heavenly horses " taken to China from Ferghana over the
Silk Route in the reign of Wu Ti, B. C. 140-86, were very
highly prized and said to be so spirited that their sweat was like
beads of blood.

The *Shih Chi* mentions Emperor Wu Ti obtaining grapes from
Ta-wan, Ferghana. The city of Han was probably the capital
of this territory.

87. TO GOVERNOR LI OF TZŬ
PREFECTURE

In the ten thousand mountain valleys, giant trees
    finger the sky;
From a thousand hills the whistle of the cuckoo echoes.
After a long night of rain
A hundred waterfalls tumble threaded spray above the
    tops of the trees . . .
The Han girls will pay tribute to you, Governor, with
    t'ung cloth;
And men of Pa will quarrel in court over their tiny plots
    of taro land.

Wên Wêng, that old scholar, turned the educational
    system upside down.
Of course you will dare to follow the old sage's
    good example?

Flowers from the t'ung tree in Szechwan were used to make
cloth. The t'ung tree may denote the cotton tree, *Salamalia*.

Wêng Wêng: a governor of Szechwan in the reign of Wu Ti.
When he discovered to his horror that the people of that province were little more than barbarians, he established schools
and invited scholars from the capital to teach. Szechwan soon
became as civilized as Ch'i and Lu (very advanced states in the
north-east of China).

88. A VIEW OF THE HAN RIVER

This mighty river rushes out beyond earth and heaven
Passing the three Hsiang cities in the Kingdom of Ch'u.
With nine tributaries flowing through the
　　gateway of Ching.
Sometimes colours play upon the mountain,
　　sometimes not . . .
Towns and cities seem to float above the
　　junction of the waters;
Great waves leap to the far skies.
Hey! You over there in Hsiang-yang! Set aside some
　　fine day
For a venerable old man of the mountains to get
　　happily drunk!

Ching-mên: a mountain in Hupeh south of the Yangtze River.
Along with Fu-ya, Tiger's Tooth Mountain, at the north it
formed a gateway or high gorge leading to the West.

Ching: an early political division, supposed to be one of the
nine provinces of Emperor Yü, B. C. 2205. It comprised Hunan,
part of Hupeh and Kueichow. It constituted the Kingdom of
Ch'u of feudal times

89. IN LATE SPRING OFFICIAL YEN AND OTHER GENTLEMEN VISIT ME

Pines and chrysanthemums adorn my three
    deserted paths;
My house is crammed with enough books and pictures
    to fill five carts.
My honourable guests came to my poor cottage to admire
    the bamboo grove;
I entertained them with roasted sunflower seeds.
Birds feed their young even before the
    spring grass greens,
And parrots shriek as they fly through falling flowers...
I pity myself with my yellowing hair.
So many years have passed—twice precious the
    time remaining!

90. FAREWELL TO CH'IU WEI

Homeward bound I ride on horseback out beyond the
    white clouds;
The mountain road zig-zags on before me.
Today and tomorrow,
I know my heart will not be at rest...
I have troubled you, a busy official, to bid me farewell;
Expect me again with the spring flowers.
At each step forward, I look back at you.
Slowly I approach the nearby pass.

91 DRIFTING IN A BOAT ALONG THE FRONT SLOPE

Far, translucent autumn sky,
How high a world above the little world of man!
I am happy just to watch a crane perched on the edge
    of the sand,
Or the far away mountains beyond the cloudlands...
The creamy waves catch the twilight
And the silver moon shines benignly down.
Tonight I set out for a lonely sail—I care not where.
Returning when? How can I decide!

92. LIFE ON THE FARM AT CH'I RIVER

I live in retirement above the waters of Ch'i River;
The eastern wilderness stretches wide—not a hill in sight!
The sun is lost behind the mulberry trees,
Little village houses dot the river bank.
An approaching shepherd boy eagerly eyes the hamlet;
Hunting dogs lag behind masters returning
    from the chase.
And what about this lonely man?
He keeps his thatched gate closed all day long.

Man Crossing a Natural Bridge, by Chang Fêng
who flourished *ca.* 1645—1670
Courtesy, C.T. Loo, New York
See poem 96

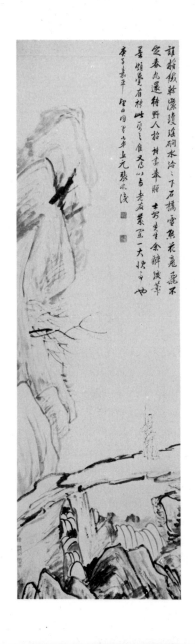

93. THOUGHTS WRITTEN ON
A WINTER NIGHT

How cold the winter evening, oh how long!
Within the palace, the water-clock drip drips
   away the night!
Without, grasses gleam white with heavy frost;
Barren trees stand stark against the clear moon.
My silken gown mocks my weather-beaten cheeks;
The lantern dyes my hair, long white, with crimson.
Now the Royal House of Han seeks young men only...
As I view my appearance, I am ashamed to
   visit my emperor!

94. TO PREMIER CHANG OF CHING-CHOU

What am I thinking today?
Sadly I look away to Ching-mên far removed ...
No one in the whole world knows me as you do.
I am reminded continually of your former kindnesses ...
I am going back to my own little farm.
There I shall arrange flowers in my rock garden.
For a long time I have had no letter from the south.
How then can I send you this message?

95. A POEM OF HAPPINESS BECAUSE TSU, THE THIRD, HAS COME TO STAY FOR THE NIGHT

A guest from Lo-yang stands before my gate !
He dismounts, brushing the dust from his garments.
I should not waste my old friend's time, coming
  to see me ;
I used to keep my door shut against visitors . . .
The heavy snow sparkles under the fading rays of the
  sun.
Travellers pass along the deep alleys ;
Among them must be some of my old friends of
  bygone days . . .
Hey !   Where are you bound for in your
  honourable carts ?

96. PASSING MONK T'AN HSIN'S MONASTERY OF THANKFUL FLOWERS

Evening ; I lean upon my bamboo staff from Szechwan,
While waiting for you at the end of Tiger Stream.
—Guests always hurry away when they hear the growl
  of the tiger in the mountains—
Following the flowing water I return to the monastery.
Clusters of wild flowers burgeon with bloom ;
How lonely the cry of the mountain bird !
I sit in solitude in this deserted village ;
The pine wind moans like fall . . .

97. LIVING LEISURELY AT WANG-CH'UAN

Since returning to White Hamlet
I have never gone back to the city's Green Gate.
Often I lean against the tree before my eaves
And look far away to the villages on the plain.
Green water plants are mirrored in the pool.
White birds wheel towards the mountains . . .
How very lonely Yü Ling-tzŭ must have been,
Hiding in the country, watering his flowers with a
  wellsweep!

Yü Ling-tzŭ : a native of the Kingdom of Ch'i in the Warring
States period, B. C. 481-221. His brother was a high official
at the court of Ch'i. Disapproving of his brother's conduct Yü
went into exile, settling at Yü Ling in the Kingdom of Ch'u.
The king of Ch'u, learning of his presence wanted to make him
premier, but Yü refused. He went into hiding and became a
gardener.

98. MY RETREAT AT MOUNT CHUNG-NAN

In middle life I became immersed in the
  philosophy of Tao ;
Later I went to live at the foot of South Mountain . . .
When I am happy I walk alone in the hills.
I know within my heart what is good and
  which is beautiful.
When I arrive at the source of the stream
I sit down to rest and to watch the mists rising.
Sometimes I meet a time-worn woodcutter—
Talking and laughing together, we forget it is time to
  go home !

99. ON AN AUTUMN EVENING IN THE MOUNTAINS

After newly-fallen rain in these vast mountains,
When evening descends the air has the feel of fall.
The limpid moon sparkles through the pine needles;
The crystal stream glides glistening over the rocks.
Babbling from the bamboo grove heralds the return of
    the washing girls.
Lotus leaves sway as the fisherman pushes along
    his sampan . . .
Although the fragrance of spring flowers has faded
My good friend, you should still stay on for the
    beauty of autumn.

100. SITTING ALONE ON AN AUTUMN NIGHT

Sitting alone, I grieve over my graying temples.
The room is empty; it is almost the second watch of
    the night.
Mountain fruit drops, drops, drops in the rain;
Insects shun the grass to chirp under my lamp.
Ah, who can restore white hair to black!
Gold cannot be made by alchemy.
Do you seek a cure for the disease of old age?
Learn then the Doctrine of Non-Being—there is the
    only remedy.

Doctrine of Non-Being: a Buddhist concept.

101. ON PASSING THE GRAVE OF CH'IN SHIH HUANG TI

His ancient grave transmuted to a grassy
   mountain peak—
A lonely sepulchre, like his ancient palace of the
   Purple Tower—
Shines with the light of sun, moon and seven stars
   from above;
While rivers, streams and the Nine Springs ripple below.
The ocean still rolls on, but no youths and maidens will
   be sent over it again.
Without the spring, no wild geese will return . . .
The plaintive music of the wind in the pines
Mourns as if his noblemen still mourned him there.

According to the *Shih Chi*, Emperor Shih Huang Ti, founder
of the Ch'in Dynasty (B. C. 221–207), was much influenced by
Taoist superstitions. During his reign he sent an expedition of
one thousand young men and women to three fairy islands in
the eastern sea to seek for pills of immortality. After his death
the Emperor was buried on Li Mountain in a vast mausoleum.
"Upon the floor, which had a foundation of bronze, was a map
of the Empire with rivers of quick-silver, the roof was studded
with constellations."

102. WATCHING THE HUNT

The General hunts near the city of Wei ;
His horn-headed arrows whine shrilly in the fierce wind.
Withered, the grass—sharp, the eagle's eye ;
Melted the snow, swift the horses' light hoofs.
Passing by chance through Hsin-fêng market,
While returning to the barracks of Hsi-liu,
I look back at the scene—there a vulture,
    shot with an arrow . .
For a thousand miles the evening clouds lie level with
    the horizon.

Wei : a city northwest of Ch'ang-an.

103 ARRIVING AT HUA-CHOU, I LOOK
ACROSS THE RIVER TO LI-YANG AND
REMEMBER TING YÜ, THE THIRD

Across the water I can glimpse the mulberry trees—
How magnificent, this Li-yang River !
Fascinated by the beckoning scenery, I am lured farther
    and farther away.
There—a solitary peak wreathed in clouds and mists . . .
Ah, never shall I see my old friend again !
The river flows peacefully, endlessly onward.
Still I rejoice ; his just fame as an administrator spreads
    so far and wide
That I sometimes overhear travellers paying him tribute.

104. SAILING ON THE RIVER
TO CH'ING-HO

Sailing on the great river
The gathered waters reach to the very rim of heaven.
Suddenly the sky-high waves part,
Disclosing country of a thousand and cities of ten
    thousand roofs.
And sailing further, still other villages and
    market-towns appear
Mid mulberry trees and growing flax.
Looking back towards my native village ...
The vast waters have joined the clouds .

Ch'ing-ho : present Ch'ing-ho Hsien, Hopei province.

105. WALKING IN THE MOUNTAINS
IN THE RAIN

A sudden shower leadens the atmosphere ;
The sky bears down upon me.
In the gloomy mountains, I catch only lightning flashes.
On the far sea, infant clouds are born.
As I ford the spring, the waters are rising in flood;
Smothering mists still cling along the precipice ...
Then the clouds quickly disperse, the rain ceases and
    moonlight gilds the river.
I hear the echoing songs of boatmen even in the depths
    of these mountains.

106. RETURNING HOME TO WANG-CH'UAN COTTAGE

The tolling of a distant bell floats faintly into the valley;
The fishermen and woodcutters gradually disappear.
Slowly the far mountains fade into darkness
Though the eastern plateau still glimmers with the
  colour of spring grass.
Vines and water chestnuts bow down before the
  tearing wind
And willow catkins dance lightly about.
Alone, I turn homeward toward beckoning white clouds.
In a mood deep with melancholy I close my
  thatched door.

107. COMPOSED WHILE ASCENDING P'EI TI'S SMALL TERRACE

Dwelling here quietly, why should I ever leave home?
One can always fill his eyes with clouds and mountains.
Across the falling sun, the weary birds slant westward
  beyond the horizon.
In this sere wilderness, far from the hustling world, men
  live in leisure.
The eaves of my cottage are hidden
From those on the edge of the distant forest.
Still, good friend, I find magic in a moonlit stroll,
So look to your door and leave it open!

108. TO THE MASTER OF THOUSAND PAGODA RESIDENCE

A sumptuous festival fills the inn with gaiety;
Passenger boats are lured thither by lights and music.
Below the windows prattle the waters of Pien River,
And the boats of the men of Ch'u sail slowly past the door.
Chickens and dogs clutter the village lanes;
On the distant fields elm and mulberry shadows cast long patterns.
The master of Thousand Pagodas has not yet made his appearance,
But smoky clouds of steam mattress his house—like bedding!

109. AFTER BEING DEMOTED AND SENT TO CHI-CHOU

How easy for a lowly official to become tangled in the net of law!
Now, demoted, I am exiled south of the Chi River.
There arrogant officers correct the culprit harshly.
The wise Emperor may not have had this in mind.
Houses march monotonously along the irrigated fields.
A sea of thick cloud rolls over the village.
Even if I should ever return,
These lonely grief-crushed years will have stolen the hair from my temples . . .

Chi-chou: a city in Shantung Province.

110. *LIVING IN THE MOUNTAINS*

I close my thatched door on my aloneness.
How very few call at my humble dwelling!
The blue arch of heaven pales behind long
   rays of sunset,
And cranes nest in every scented pine . . .
Now tender bamboo shoots are coated with fresh powder;
And around the lotus lie fallen crimson petals.
At the ferry landing, lights spring up
And peasants, laden with water-chestnuts, gather from
   hither and yon.

111. *THOUGHTS ON SEEING MÊNG HAO-JAN, THE SIXTH, OFF TO HSIANG-YANG*

I bar my door: I do not want to go out.
For a long time now I have stayed at home
   with my thoughts.
Yes, this is the best plan:
Let me urge you also to return to your old retreat,
Where, drunk on country wine, we shall sing,
And smile when reading aloud from the Classics!
That is the way to live!
It banishes the longing for dreams, the haunting ghosts
   of earth-bound life!

POEMS OF EIGHT
SEVEN-CHARACTER LINES

112-115

112. WRITTEN IN THE MOUNTAINS IN EARLY FALL

Without talent, who dares burden so brilliant an era!
Today my thoughts turn toward the east river where I
  still keep my old retreat . . .
Do I condemn Shang P'ing who married off his children
  early?
Or disagree with T'ao Ch'ien who retired too late?
Crickets chirp urgently among the grasses as fall
  hurries past.
In the mountains the desolate cry of the cicadas disturbs
  the dusk.
No longer do people stop at my deserted gate.
I am left alone with white clouds in this empty forest.

113. *A REPLY TO CHIA CHIH, A COURT OFFICIAL, ON A MORNING LEVEE AT THE PALACE OF GREAT BRILLIANCE*

Proudly the purple hooded cock-man proclaims the arrival of dawn.

The Warden of Robes enters accompanying the cloud-blue imperial furs.

The nine " gates of heaven " swing open on the palace courts within;

Worshipping officials from ten thousand countries kneel before the imperial insignia.

The first rays of the sun gild the " fairy palms ";

Smoke of incense swirls round the dragons writhing on each royal robe—they seem to float among the clouds.

After the morning levee, you will write the five-coloured edicts;

Then, to the jingle of jades and gems, go proudly toward your home at the edge of Phoenix Pool.

The cock-man: a palace official who announced the break of day, literally, that the cock had crowed!

" Gates of heaven ": because heaven was supposed to have nine gates, so the imperial palace on earth had the same.

Emperor Wu Ti, B.C. 140–86, had erected before his palace two columns on which were placed fairy palms to collect dew for making the pill of immortality.

In the T'ang Dynasty different colours of paper were used for edicts, according to their importance.

Smoke curls slowly upward in these deserted mountains
after days of desolate rain.

Again the hellebore and the millet are cooked for
labourers on the land to the east.

Above the speading rice-fields a white egret stretches
its wings,

And golden orioles sing within the dark foliage of
summer trees . . .

I practise quietism among these solitary hills and, musing
upon the morning hibiscus, think upon life.

Under the pines I live frugally, munching dewy sunflower seeds,

A wild old man of the mountain, long past desire to
compete for official promotion . . .

Now what right have my only neighbours, the sea gulls,
to be shy of me!

The morning hibiscus blooming but a day, was symbolic of the
brevity of life.

Gilded with sun-set, the towers of your mansion
  are aflame.

Blossoms of peach and plum brighten the purple shade;
  willow catkins sail in the air.

From within the forbidden halls, the distant bell rings
  out the end of day for office workers.

A few executives linger on . . .
  Birds begin their good-night lullaby;

At daybreak, you hasten to the golden palace, your jade
  decorations bouncing;

At evening, with a deep court bow, you receive the edict
  from the Emperor . . .

Once I wanted to follow your course, but now, afflicted
  with years

And resigned to fate, I put away official robes—and rest.

IRREGULAR POEMS
FIVE-CHARACTER LINES

116-131

116. A FAREWELL

On your departure I dismount, and drink to your health.
I ask : "Where are you going?"
You say, "I have not found the voice of my heart;
So I shall return to my hermitage in the foothills of the
    Southern Mountain : there I shall find rest.
There, no one asks the reason for my leaving . . .
There, white clouds sail on forever without
    exhausting time."

117. IN A BAMBOO TEA-HOUSE ON A SPRING NIGHT WHEN, UPON OFFICIAL CH'IEN'S RETURN TO LAN-T'IEN, I PRESENT HIM WITH THIS POEM

A quiet night, all living things are still.
Only the lonely bark of a dog echoes from beyond the
    forest.
I understand . . . I, too, once lived in the mountains
Remote from the families west of the river at the foot of
    the gorge.
I envy you ! At dawn you will start your pilgrimage,
A simple hermit plucking herbs, freed of ambition for
    the security of an official coronet !

Reluctant night spreads lingering twilight across the
forgotten village;
Cattle and sheep wind homeward through the
narrow lanes.
Leaning heavily on his staff, the old peasant waits beside
his thatched door;
He worries over his tardy shepherd son . . .
Strutting pheasants call in the rich young wheat fields;
Silkworms slumber; few mulberry leaves remain.
Hoes slung across shoulders, farmers clump along home,
And meeting their fellows, loiter to chatter incessantly. . .
I long for their leisure and sense of ease!
I try to hide my envy by humming the old
song of Shih-wei!

Shih-wei : title of a poem in the *Shih Ching*.
"How few of us are left, how few!
Why do you not go back?"
Ref. Waley, Book of Songs. p. 113.

119. GREEN RIVER

When we go to Yellow Flower Spring,
We usually follow the winding path which wriggles
Along Green River and through the hills in
ten thousand turns.
As the crow flies, less than thirty miles.
The bubbling boisterous water roars among
scattered rocks;
There is the colour of tranquility in these
deep green pines.

Water chestnuts and gipsy weeds float idly on the water
Reflecting the slashing knives of reeds and rushes . . .
My heart is pure white as silk—at rest
Like this still and placid stream.
I'm going to stay on this large flat rock
And fish! That's all I desire.

Yellow Flower Spring flowed by Fêng-Hsien, Shensi Province.
Because Fêng-Hsien was called Yellow Flower Hsien in the T'ang
Dynasty the river was given that name.

120. *I STAY OVERNIGHT AT CHÊNG-CHOU*

In the morning I say goodbye to the people of Chou;
In the evening I arrive at Chêng.
Having no friends elsewhere along the way,
The lonely traveller makes a companion of his
    servant boy.
I keep looking for Nan-yang and Lo-yang; I cannot
    see them;
Autumn rain, falling steadily, darkens the plain.
Old farmers turn homeward from their fields on the edge
    of the grasslands.
Village youngsters herd their cattle in the rain.
Their master lives on the eastern plateau
Where the crops are piled high about his thatched house.
Insects chirp sadly under the loom
And bird-songs come from the ripened grain . . .
Well, tomorrow I must cross the river Ching.
Last night I travelled the long road from the
    Pass of Gold.
Why am I doing this?
To seek a government position with a small salary on
    some remote edge of the world.

121. *PASSING LI YI'S COTTAGE*

His lonely gate is the colour of ripened grass;
No carriage, no horse has stopped there the
    whole day long.
When guests do invade this dark forbidding alley,
Dogs bark behind his bamboo fence.
With hair unkempt—What? bother about hair-pins?—
He strolls along, still holding his book of Tao . . .
Here is a man after my own heart,
Content with poverty, to seek undistracted, Truth.
We quaff a glass of the good wine of Yi-ch'êng,
Then I weave my way back to the Buddhist
    monastery at Lo-yang.

122. *A SONG OF HSI-SHIH*

Since beauty rates so highly everywhere under Heaven,
How could Hsi-shih remain long undiscovered!
One morning, only a lowly girl washing silk in the
    Yüeh River;
By evening, raised to Imperial Concubine at the Royal
    Palace of Wu.
When poor, she seemed no different from other
    pretty girls,
Once famous, how men marvelled at her rarity!
Now maids all her own scent her body with
    fragrant powder
And wrap silken robes around her.
As the king's favourite she soon becomes spoiled, deve-
    lops an arrogant manner.
Protected by his love, no silly "right and wrong"
    for her!

When she haughtily deigns to visit her native village not
  one of her former silk-washing friends
May hope to ride in her grand carriage beside her;
How futile for those simple village girls
To keep imitating her charming frowns! How could
  theirs be " exceptional " like hers!

Hsi-shih: the most beautiful girl in the Kingdom of Yüeh (now
Chekiang Province) during the Warring States period, B. C.
481—221. Suffering from heart attacks, when ill she frowned,
but even this was charming. So girls of the neighbourhood
kept imitating her frowns, but instead of becoming more attrac-
tive they became the laughing stock of the community.

123. OCCASIONAL COMPOSITIONS: SIX POEMS

I.

A madman in the Kingdom of Ch'u
Never used his head to think seriously about anything.
Hair floating in the wind, wearing neither hat nor sash
He would wander along the southern path singing.
Even Confucius conversing with him
Could not inspire ideas of benevolence or righteousness.
Self-sufficient, he felt no need to ask advice from Heaven;
Why should he strike the ground with a hoe!
And how he laughed at the recluses who
  gathered herbs—
What was the sense in a man becoming a hermit!

Madman of Ch'u: Chieh Yü. See poem 78.
Ch'u included most of the present provinces of Hupeh and
Hunan.
The recluses who gathered herbs: Pê-yi and Shu chi of the
Shang Dynasty. When Wu Wang, founder of the Chou Dynasty,
conquered the Shang, he tried to persuade these two men to
become officers at his court. They refused and retired to the
mountains. They lived on herbs, but finally died of starvation.

II.

In his farm-house lives a venerable old patriarch.

Waves of white hair break on his shoulders. Content
with meagre resources,

His short coarse woolen covering never strikes him as
poor,

And with him no beauty can compare with the golden
faces of his own sunflowers.

Sometimes when his daily chores are done

He calls his neighbours in to share a flask of wine.

Under his grass-thatched eaves, mid clamour and
hubbub

His guests stand around, sit, stand again.

He never ventures forth so far as the market town, much
less the city,

But on his brief outings his eldest son, or his grandson,
escorts him in filial duty.

In ancient times the Five Emperors and the Three Kings

Were styled the Sons of Heaven.

Yet sometimes even they quarrelled, and then were
reconciled—

How then can one unlettered distinguish right from
wrong!

When we have gained the heart's desire, we should enjoy
ourselves.

There is no disgrace in liking to live in the country.

Going our way, with a free spirit,

We should follow our destiny happily, peacefully forward,
until we have shed our last tooth!

Five Emperors of the Mythological Period: Fu Hsi, Shen Nung,
Huang Ti, Yao and Shun. The Three Kings: King of Heaven,
King of Earth, King of Man.

III.

Each dawn, each dusk I longingly look toward T'ai-hang
    mountain range.
I hesitate to admit it—I have never been there.
Should you ask the reason,
I can only reply that the net of this world has
    ensnared me.
My little sister daily grows into womanhood,
My brothers have not yet married,
My family is in poverty—my salary so minute!
In all my life I have never been able to save one cash.
Many a time I have thought of seeking a better position,
But my timid mind walks forward and backward, and
    ending—backward,
Ever bewildered, not knowing which course to choose ...
The Terrace of Shen Teng, the loud-whistling hermit,
Still lures me to that shelter of pines and bamboo ...
No, it would not take too long to go there,
To my old friend, a philosopher of the Middle Way.
But the pull of my deep emotions daily slackens,
Because my desire for quiet meditation daily
    becomes stronger.
Sometime I shall rouse myself and quickly flee this
    stifling grind and turn hermit.
How much better than stagnating here until the dreary
    years are too far spent!

T'ai-hang: a mountain range in southern Shansi.
Shen Teng: a hermit who would speak to no one. He whist-
led so loudly in high mountains that it caused the hills to
vibrate.

IV.

T'ao Ch'ien followed his natural leaning—
His temperament too fond of wine.
After he resigned his official position
He was too poor to afford the fruits of the grape.
On the Ninth-day-of-the-ninth-month Festival
His empty hands held only chrysanthemums!
Deep in his heart he kept hoping—
Surely someone would bring him a little wine.
Like magic, a friend clad in white approached with a
    whole jugful and cup.
Certainly it was for this old fellow!
Yes, sir! How wildly joyous he was, gulping that wine!
What cared he whether or not he would eat.
Flinging his hat, then his palm-fibre coat into a
    deserted field,
"At least for today," he sighed with relief, "there shall
    be no worry for me to carry on my back!"
Quite dignified and proud when sober, now he could not
    tell east from west,
Nor recall where he had thrown off his clothes.
Merrily drunk, he still forced himself to keep on stag-
    gering
Toward his home at Five Willows, singing at the top of
    his lungs.
He slunk in, without asking a word about family affairs;
He must have felt thoroughly ashamed in front of
    his wife!

V.

The girl from Chao can pluck a guitar;
And dance the Han-tan also.
Yet her husband, a flippant fellow,
Wastes his time on fighting cocks while serving the
    King of Ch'i,
Spending yellow gold to buy songs and smiles
    from courtesans!
He squanders money without counting it.
Relatives of the emperor, Hsü and Shih, frequent
    his home.
Four horses often paw the ground before his great gate;
In his guest hall he retains a Confucian scholar,
One so learned as to rank half-way between Mencius
    and Confucius.
For all of thirty years this sage has broused among books
But ever refused the yard of silk of officialdom,
Even though poverty haunted him all his life—
Too true to the teachings of the ancient sages.

Han-tan: the capital of the state of Chao, the present Han-tan
Hsien in Hopeh Province.

Ch'i: modern Shantung.

VI.

Buried beneath so many years—I am grown too lazy to
  compose poems,
Completely smothered with the sense of being old!
I know I am admired as a poet,
Yet in some former life, surely I was a great painter
Since I still cannot suppress my deep inclination
  toward art.
Too, I am considered an artist by common men—at
  least at times.
Though not for any pictures—only my name—
How little, oh how very little they understand what lies
  within my heart!

124. *WEEPING OVER THE DEATH
      OF YIN YAO*

How long may a man expect to live?
Soon or late, he must again become nothingness...
As I sit here brooding over your death,
Ten thousand memories sadden my heart...
Your beloved mother's body is not yet buried;
And your little girl is only ten years old...
Over the vast and lonely countryside
I hear the desolate sound of weeping.
Drifting clouds blot out the blue of Heaven;
Flying birds no longer call...
How melancholy must the lone traveller be!
Even in the busy day I am crushed with grief...
I remember while you were still with us,
You asked me to teach you the Principle of the Void.

Alas, that I never did instruct you!
Your failure to attain the goal—my fault, not yours.
Former friends have each presented their funeral gifts—
But oh, why not have given them while you were living!
And I? I have shown you ingratitude in more ways
   than one ...
Weeping bitterly, I go blindly to my own humble door.

125. A MEAL FOR A MONK FROM MOUNT FU-FU

Though late in life, now I understand clearly the Prin-
   ciple of Quietism:
Daily to keep far away from swarming men.
I shall wait for the monk from the distant mountain.
Having already swept the path before my small house
   for his coming,
Surely he will descend from those clouds hiding the
   mountain peak
To visit my thatched hut.
With pine needles and grasses I cook rice;
Beside incense tapers I read my book of Tao.
Then I light my lamp when the day is almost done.
How quickly I have experienced the deep peace
   born of quietness!
This contemplative life blesses one with an abundance
   of leisure ...
Why should you think so seriously of returning?
This worldly life with all its affairs is empty and void.

Principal of Quietism: a Taoist concept.

General Li of the Han Dynasty
Sprang from three generations of generals.
While his hair was still kotted in childhood, he proved
    clever at strategy.
In the prime of his manhood he was strong and brave.
He drove the Tartars far from the frontier,
Hotly pursuing them to the innermost tents of the Khan
Where royal flags and banners fluttered close-ranked
    as soldiers.
All through the night, on the very edge of the desert,
Fierce was the noise of battle, choked with smoke and
    blinding dust.
How mournful now the defeated sound of enemy flutes
    and drums!
Merely to serve his illustrious prince at court was not
    enough for him—
He would annihilate those proud barbarians!
Then sudden humiliation! Losing contact with his
    main forces
He suffered the indignity of capture by the Mongols.
He, who has basked in the Imperial Favour since
    early youth—
Now imprisoned, alone, how could he bear think of
    that now?
His whole thought became one great resolution—some-
    how still to repay his Prince with gratitude.
Eagerly he had risked his life, but the privilege of death
    was denied him.

Continually he strained his eyes toward the horizon
 hoping to see his far-away friend Tzŭ-ch'ing coming.
Who else had the empathy to understand his plight?

127. A FAREWELL TO SECRETARY CH'I-MU WHO, RETIRING FROM OFFICE, IS LEAVING FOR EAST OF THE YANGTZE

In this most illustrious period of our era, you stagnate
 in a humble position.
I, also, have been likewise ignored.
This is our lot, so why wear the face of mourning!
Life still holds the "white silk" of integrity.
As I reflect on your fate, official robe exchanged for the
 garments of exile,
I wonder what next can happen within the Four Seas!
For ten thousand miles the autumn sky lies empty even
 of clouds;
Long rays from the sunset light up the broad river.
How deep the quiet night . . .
Perhaps you are even now beating the side of your small
 boat in time to moonlight singing,
Wisely hiding your talents away from men, among fish
 and birds.

Be tranquil then, like water trickling through duckweed
   and clumps of rushes...
We need not travel in the glitter of that bright world,
Which daily only frosts our worn-out temples more the
   colour of frozen grass.
Happily stupid, what do I know of the clamouring
   events of the world,
A rustic dwelling far from the sage Emperor!
Even were my simple advice to be followed,
Who could judge if it be right or wrong?
No, like you, I also left officialdom
To cultivate the good earth like an old farmer, my
   friend.

128. *FAREWELL TO CH'I-WU CH'IEN WHO
      IS RETURNING TO HIS HOME AFTER
      FAILING HIS EXAMINATIONS*

There are no hermits in this age of enlightenment—
Now "flowering spirits" crowd to serve at court!
Thus you, too, native of the Eastern Hills
Were lured to leave the solitary life of herb-gathering.
Still, had you attained the golden gate of your dreams
Who then would say that avid ambition was wrong?
Somewhere between the Yangtze and the Huai you
   spent the Festival-of-the-cold-Meal;
And between the capital and Lo-yang you stitched your
   spring apparel.

Now you turn homeward from Ch'ang-an; we bring out
  wine to bid you farewell.
Kindred spirit, now our ways must separate.
You will float lightly along on cinnamon oars.
Too soon you will reach your own thatched door;
The distant woods will have compassed your
  familiar way;
The silent city wall will gleam welcome in the dusky sun.
Although your ambition failed of fulfilment,
Never doubt but one friend knows the mournful music
  of your soul!

According to a story in the Book of *Lieh Tzŭ*, Po-ya was an
expert on the lute, Chung Tzŭ-ch'i, an expert listener. When
Po-ya thought of a high mountain while playing, Tzŭ-ch'i would
immediately say: "How mighty and lofty it sounds! You are
thinking about a high mountain." Or when Po-ya thought of
running water Tzŭ-ch'i would remark "How smooth and
pleasant! Your thought is on running water!" When Chung
died, Po-ya never played his lute again; who else could ever
understand his music? Hence the phrase "know music" came
to signify deep understanding.

129. TO P'EI TI

We have not seen each other—
We have not seen each other for a long time.
At the source of the stream, day after day,
I recall how we used to clasp hands—
Hand in hand, eye to eye—because we had the
  same heart . . .
How I grieved when you left so unexpectedly!
That is the way I feel towards you even today—
This mutual love, then—is it deep? Or not!

130. *TO MY BROTHER, TS'UI CHI-CHUNG OF P'U-YANG, RECALLING OUR ENJOYMENT OF THE DISTANT MOUNTAIN IN FRONT OF OUR GATE*

The riotous red leaves put us in high spirits—
Also the fact that you lived leisurely here
Quietly, within the western forest,
Your own familiar mountain towers before the gate ...
Now the ineffable blue of distance floats between us
    across a thousand miles.
A few peaks pierce the lowering clouds.
Cliffs and jagged precipices face the Kingdom of Ch'in
And lofty ranges hide the Ching pass.
Sun rays slant through scattered showers,
And flying birds are folded into the twilight
    mountain mists.
That is how my old friend lives today ...
I sigh at the sight of my own ravaged, worn-out face.

Ch'in: Shensi-Kansu area.

131. *THREE POEMS OF FOUR WISE MEN OF CH'I-CHOU*

I. Secretary Ts'ui

Relinquishing his official seal, he retired to his peaceful
    farm at the foot of East Mountain.
How wise, this sagely man!
Public spirited in youth,
In age he withdrew from the world

To the foot of East Mountain; there he became a Con-
fucian scholar,
And lived by the shore of the timeless sea.
For recreation, I hear, he played with the birds.
Oh, to sail out with him on his raft!

Confucius: "If I sail on a raft in the sea (become a hermit),
one of my followers must be Yü (a disciple of his)." Chang
Liang, a great statesman, set "sail on a raft" after he had helped
Liu Pang establish himself as first emperor of the Han Dynasty
B. C. 206—A.D. 220.

II.   Literati Ch'êng

Gorgeous in garments worth a thousand gold, sporting a
gem-decked sword,
You ascended to the white jade guest hall of the Prince
Who honoured you, as guests were honoured in the
palace of Prince P'ing Yüan.
You kept the most seductive courtesans of Han-tan;
Could consult at whim even the exalted and powerful,
bearing the seals of dukes and nobles;
You were privileged to share secrets with
roaming knight-errants.
Yet for all your worldly treasures, you never found the
desire of your heart;
You escaped into illness and ran away to be a guest at
the court of Liang.

Prince P'ing Yüan: of the State of Chao in the Warring States
Period, B.C. 481—221. Rich and generous, he entertained
hundreds of guests in his palace without knowing who they
were. However with the aid of these guests he was able to
save his country from an attack by neighbouring states.

III. Two Men of the Mountain, Chêng and Huo

All the handsome dandies of the community
Belonged to two clans, Chin and Chang.
Lucky for them, they inherited wealth from their parents
And from childhood they were protected by
    Imperial Favour.
In their youth they shunned all study,
Competing with one another only for rich viands and
    sumptuous mansions...
Now Chêng and Huo were eminently fitted to be in-
    cluded among the literati,
But no one cared to introduce them to his majesty.
Master Chêng grew old with the streams and rocks;
Huo, the younger, dwelt quietly among the hills.
Honest men, they sold herbs without two prices;
Illustrious men, they wrote books of more than ten
    thousand characters;
Good men, they disdained "refuge under trees of
    wicked reputation"
And drank water only from clear springs.
I am not worthy of mention
But men such as these, well, who more important can
    we discuss?

According to *Kuan Tzŭ*, a good man should never rest under the
shade of trees of wicked reputation—associate with evil men.

IRREGULAR POEMS
SEVEN-CHARACTER LINES

132-136

132. A POEM SENT TO A
CH'UNG-FAN MONK

Ch'ung-fan Monk! Ch'ung-fan Monk!
When autumn comes to Fu-fu village, spring will have
    long disappeared.
Falling flowers and crying birds—what confusion!
But not in the mountain window of the river valley
    house—there lonely quiet reigns.
In this shut-in hamlet, who knows or cares about events
    in the world outside?
In the distant city people look enviously at the quiet
    cloud-capped mountain.

133. ANSWERING CHANG, THE
FIFTH BROTHER

In Chung-nan stands a small cottage
Opposite a mountain with the same name.
Front door closed—the whole year passed
    without a guest.
My heart is at ease all day long,
So where is the harm in drinking wine and fishing?
As for you, you may come when you come and go when
    you wish.

In the house across the street lives a maiden from
 Lo-yang,
Tender with youth, perhaps fifteen years—or a
 little more.
Her maids serve her delectable carp on a golden platter.
Everyone can see her painted towers, her
 vermilion pavilions,
Gracefully draped with peach trees and green willows.
When she emerges from her private chamber she is
 ushered into a coach redolent with seven fragrances.
Jewelled fans welcome her return to her nine-flowered
 curtained apartment.
Her lover, rich and noble, audacious and dauntless, in
 the springtime of his youth,
Controls his steed with a bridle set with jade.
How he swaggers! His boastful airs outdo even those
 of Chi-lun!
And he likewise lavishly bestows upon his friends pre-
 cious coral trees.
He loves his maiden with the passion of Ju-nan for his
 famed concubine, Green Jade. He teaches her to
 dance.
They are never through playing together until the breeze
 of the glimmering dawn blows out
The "nine mystic candles" behind the
 spring-sweet window
Leaving spirals of violet smoke in flowery wisps.
She has no time to practise songs,

Elegantly dressed, delicately perfumed, she waits for him
the whole day long ...

But from morning till night he goes from the homes of
the Chaos to the houses of the Lis,

To his boon companions in town, likewise wealthy and
nobly born.

Who now would pity the girl from Yüeh River with a
face like translucent jade

Who when poor and humble washed silk at the source
of the stream!

Chi-lun, also known as Shih Ch'ung: the wealthiest man in the
Chin Dynasty, third and fourth century A. D. He presented
costly coral trees to his friends.

Emperor Wu Ti of the Han Dynasty, when waiting for the
Queen Mother of the Western Heavens had nine mystic candles
lighted.

The girl from Yüeh River: Hsi-Shih, See poem 122.

As a boy in his teens, say between fifteen and twenty,
The old general had chased and subdued a wild Mongol
horse, proudly riding it away.
With one arrow he had killed a white-crowned tiger in
the mountains,
And, equalling the skill of Yellow Beard from
South Yeh,
Alone he had patrolled and defended a thousand miles
of desert
And single-handed had withstood a million men!
His spirited troops from Han, terrible and swift as
thunder and lightning,
Struck terror into the retreating Tartar cavalry, paralyzed
by his terrible weapon, the caltrop...
Wei Ch'ing never knew defeat—his destined luck
from Heaven;
Li Kuang never knew victory—his destined
tragic misfortune...
Old at last, fibre softened like decaying wood,
His hair long-since turned snow from so dangerous a
life, the general retired.
Once his perfect archery had never missed the bird's eye.
But cursed with age, of what use is he now! His weak
left elbow droops like a willow branch.
So he sells mellons beside the road like that
Marquis of old,
And imitating T'ao Ch'ien, plants willows to shade
his door.

All the little houses in the poor alleys are linked by dark
  trees older than he.
A solitary mountain stares into his empty window . . .
But still he is determined to command the rushing
  waters of Su-lê.
What? Let himself go like the general of Ying-ch'uan
  ever befuddled by wine? Not he!
Suddenly beneath the Honan mountain armies gather
  like foreboding clouds.
From morning till night urgent messages are heard
  exchanged;
Officers recruit young men from the
  Three-river Provinces.
Then five successive imperial orders are sent to the
  old general:
Laboriously he polishes his worn metal armour until,
  the years rolled back, it glitters again the
  steel-blue of ice.
Proudly he brandishes his precious sword, flashing it
  through the air like a falling star.
How he longs for a bow of Yen to shoot the
  barbarian general!
He would die of shame should the clash of armies
  trouble the ears of his Emperor.
Never despise this old hero from Yün-chung—
His spirit shall carry him through yet one more battle
  to defend his brilliant record!

Yellow Beard: nickname for Ts'ao Chang, a son of the famous
general Ts'ao Ts'ao of the Three Kingdoms, (A. D. 220–265).

Wei Ch'ing and Li Kuang   distinguished generals in the Han Dynasty, B. C. 206—A. D. 220.

According to legend when Chih Li-shu and Hua Chiai-shu went up a mountain to watch the sun rise they found suddenly that willow trees were growing under their left arms. The arms later became useless.

The Marquis of Tung-ling, in the Ch'in Dynasty, B. C. 221—205, becoming a poor man after the fall of the Dynasty, planted mellons east of Ch'ang-an to earn his living. Because of their fine flavour they were called Mellons of the Former Marquis.

In the Later Han Dynasty Kêng Kung was appointed general to fight the Tartars. At the city of Su-lê he found the only source of fresh water for his troops. He hurriedly took the city and spring, but the Tartars cut off the access to the water. Becoming desperate Kêng prayed by a well for water. Suddenly rushing streams burst out of the earth.

Kuan Fu, the general of Ying-ch'uan   noted for his arrogance, violence and addiction to wine.

The Three-river Provinces   Hotung Hopei, and Honan.

Yen, present province of Hopei: famous for producing bows and arrows.

Yün-chung   a county in Shansi Province. The general referred to was Wei Shang.

According to legend when Hou Yi and Wu Ho were travelling northward, Wu asked Hou to shoot the left eye of a bird with his arrow. Hou Yi shot but instead of hitting the left, shot the right eye. Hou Yi felt ashamed of this all the rest of his life.

The fisherman loved those mountains in spring; often
his boat curved the course of the river.

Blossoming peach trees lined with pink the banks
of the old stream,

And he, sitting in his boat, bewitched by the beauty of
the red flowers forgot both time and space.

Drifting along one day to the very end of the river,
suddenly he saw people.

Quietly beaching his boat he was lured by a deep winding cavern.

Then darkness gave way to light and level land lay
shining before him.

Beyond in the hazy blue he could faintly descry a forest
crowned by a crest of clouds,

And drawing near he noticed, amazed, a thousand homes
scattered mid flowers and feathers of bamboo groves.

He heard woodcutters mentioning names belonging to
men in the Han Dynasty !

And the people still wore clothing in the style of
Ch'in.

They were all living together along the Wu-ling River,

Tilling their rice fields and gardens—a veritable
fairyland.

At night their sleeping houses were patterned by
moonlight filtered through pines ;

At dawn when the sun began to break through the
clouds, cocks crowed and dogs barked . . .

Surprised by the arrival of this strange visitor, the
people hurried to gather round him ;

They jostled one another to invite him to their homes to
ply him with questions : Where had he come from ?
What was his home like ?

Early each morning they swept away the flower petals
in the alleyways before their houses to welcome him;

Early each evening woodcutters came in along the river
to visit him ...

Seeking a refuge from the chaos of life they had left
the world of men.

Wishing to imitate the Immortals, now they would
never return.

Within this cave they knew nothing of the haste and
alarums in the hard real world.

People outside the cave saw only the cloud-capped mountain far away ...

The fisherman was not sure that this fairy land might
ever be reached again.

His love of the world fought the temptation to stay—
he still longed for his native village.

Thus he left the cave, thinking that no matter how far
beyond mountain and river he must travel

Some day he would say farewell to his home, and return
to enchantment to wander about for a much
longer time.

He thought he would remember the way—

But who would have guessed that mountains and valleys
could shift like clouds—all changed !

He could only recall entering that deep mountain—

Several times he followed the blue stream, his eyes on
the cloud forest, but always, always in vain.

With spring, the rising Peach Flower Stream
 flowed everywhere.
He could no longer tell in which direction to seek this
 Fairy land.

Han Dynasty: B.C. 206—A.D. 220.
Ch'in Dynasty: B.C. 221—. 207.